MAXIMIZE

7 MIND-SHIFTS THAT WILL HELP YOU MAXIMIZE KEY AREAS OF YOUR LIFE

HENRY J. LUCAS, LCSW, LCADC

I dedicate this book to my amazing wife and daughter. Thank you for loving and believing in me. To my mom and mother-in-law, thank you for the life you have given. Without you, there is no "us." My sister and sister-in-law, you show me resilience and perseverance. Thanks to all the women who have guided and shaped me into the man that I am.

FOREWORD

I loved my patients. But the system, not so much. It was a revolving door and I knew they needed so much more. I needed so much more. The mundane routine of the 9-to-5 had to stop! And one day, I decided to maximize MY potential. I decided to create a program that invested in the lives of others in a way no other program has. This, in turn, gave me purpose and allowed me to express the passion I felt and start living a life worth living. It was in the beginning of this journey that I met Henry. We were both eager professionals, looking for a way to connect to those that are ready to pour into those afflicted by mental illness and addiction.

My passion stems from growing up in "the rooms" with my father, Michael T. White, affectionately known as "Mike White." He passed in away in 2016 after his battle with cancer. During his life, he made an incredible impact on the world of recovery and especially, my life. His recovery propelled me through 12 years of medical training and inspired a passion for helping those who are struggling with addiction. He left me his legacy to carry on. I was afraid and intimidated by the tasks of fighting addiction in the West End of Louisville Kentucky. But with the wisdom he instilled in me and the amazingly loyal people he touched, we have been able to carry forth the mission, in his spirit. The seeds he planted, very purposefully, are blooming. This is the type of passion Henry speaks of in his book. He gives you the recipe for taking full advantage of this life you're given.

Maximize parallels so many lessons I learned from my father. He would say, "do something for others without looking for something in return." Henry spoke of this in Chapter 6. When you're acting selflessly, it creates a culture of caring that spreads through all members of the community. Learn how this concept can not only impact those around you but live by these words and watch it change your life as well.

When I met Henry, I immediately noticed his sincere demeanor, accompanied with his obvious expertise in the field, and this led me to request him to develop the substance abuse curriculum for my clinic. The curriculum has been a guide for our therapists and a life-saving tool for our patients. This book is just another example of watching the author walk his talk. We have served as inspiration to one another and this is no different. Careful, as his maximizing spirit is infectious! Your new life awaits.

Teresa Walker, M.D.
Owner/Founder of New Leaf Clinic
www.newleaf1216.com

INTRO

I have searched throughout my entire life to find a solution to the title of this book. Being the youngest of two, I'm naturally selfish. My life has revolved around getting "the most." As an American millennial raised in a society and culture of "more," I developed a perspective of getting "the most." Some of you reading this may have pioneered this culture of more; I can hear some middle-aged Gen-Xer advertising dude promising, "this (product or service) will give you more bang for your buck." *More bang for your buck.* Now there's a phrase that encapsulates most of our culture. We want something phenomenal for the least amount of money and effort. The technology age and its advances have made humanity lazy – well maybe just first-world humanity. Everything is at our fingertips: you can watch any movie, show, lecture or concert from anywhere on the planet. That's exciting news! We can download the most current scientific data within seconds. We can search the web and find support for anything. These are incredible leaps for the modern thinker and tech whiz.

The second part of the title of this book was inspired by a sermon I heard at a loved one's funeral in 2010. She died from a lethal combination of methadone and Xanax. Separately, these two classes of drugs have the power to kill, but combined, they are known as the "Death Cocktail." These substances suppress the central nervous and respiratory systems which leads to someone not waking up. This woman's horrendous death left scars that will live forever – including the fact that her children will never know their mother. Like most funerals, hers was somber and sad, punctuated by thoughts like, "If things had only been different," and "She never reached her full potential." Have you experienced the same feelings when paying your respects at someone's funeral? The underlying meaning in these statements is, "I wish they would have maximized their time on earth."

I have sat through numerous sermons. I'm sure the one the preacher gave at my friend's funeral has been preached a thousand times in many different languages. That day, though, I felt the sermon in my bones, especially when he asked the congregation, "What is the most important thing on a tombstone?" No one answered him, but I thought it had to be the day of birth or the day of death. I would have been wrong twice. "The most important thing on the tombstone is the hyphen between birth date and death date," the preacher announced. He referred to this hyphen as a "dash" and kept asking us, "How are you going to live your dash?" The space between the birthdate and death date is our life. For some of us the "dash" may span 80 years. Sadly, for some infants, their birthdate may be their death date. But for those of us who have the "dash" – *this life* – are we maximizing our time on the planet? We never know exactly how much time is on our clock. Are we living this relatively small amount of time to its fullest potential? This book is about living a life with no regrets, experiencing the adventure of our daily lives through practical concepts, and reclaiming what's already yours—your life on this earth!

Life is funny. Life is constant. Life can be constantly funny. Life is the breath you breathe and the seed you plant; however, life can also be viewed on a time continuum. Earth has been around for billions of years and you will be here for roughly 80 years. Some of you may not live many seconds after finishing this book. Disclaimer: There is no evidence that the previous statement is true. What is my point? Recognize that your life is fragile and vulnerable but understand it's still *your* life. You've got to have some "skin in the game (of life)" – and this book challenges you to get the most out of it.

When you read and apply the wisdom within these pages, you will achieve the goal of getting the most out of you! You are an excellent investment, one that will yield an abundant return. In the pages that follow, you will be exposed to age-old concepts that have maximized lives for millennia. You deserve to transcend your limitations and barriers to live a life of fulfillment and purpose. As you read, I ask several things from you; be open-minded, "try on" or allow yourself to experience the concepts, take what you need, and leave the rest.

In the following chapters I share 10 approaches that I believe will allow you to get the most from your life. Each chapter is followed by *Shifts and Movements*, which are questions and tasks to activate each approach. This book is a guide for sustainable wellbeing, inspiration, and change. I hope it engages you and helps you transform your life.

Henry J. Lucas, LCSW, LCADC

CHAPTER 1

ATTITUDE AND PERSPECTIVE

"If you don't like something, change it. If you can't change it, change your attitude."
MAYA ANGELOU

Our attitude and perspective are the keys in getting the most from life, and there are a multitude of influential factors that shape them. For example, the "everybody-gets-a-trophy" generation can and will cultivate an attitude of entitlement and arrogance which leads to altered perspectives of reality. If I have an attitude of entitlement after I graduate from college with the expectation of obtaining gainful employment in a saturated field, then my perspective of potential employers and my career field can be hyper-critical. I can feel unworthy and victimized. Feelings of low self-worth and victimization can lead to catastrophic outcomes—substance abuse, self-harm, depression. Attitude and perspective shape the course of lives. So then, we are never in control but rather, our attitude and perspective control us and ultimately dictate our happiness.

The cliché, "Is the glass half empty or half full?" pertains to attitude and perspective. According to the cliché, people are either pessimists or optimists. I think both perspectives can add value or disruption to our lives. Pessimists may be extra cautious because they already know what the outcome is, which may prevent some loss or heartache, e.g. "He will just cheat on me like my last lover so what's the point?" This perspective can keep us safe. The optimist may say, "Even though my heart has been broken, this may have been the greatest person and relationship in the world." This type of attitude can lead to another failed relationship because it sets up an unrealistic expectation that no future person or relationship can possibly fulfill. No one will live up to this individual's perception of their "perfect" match. So, is the glass half full or half empty?

Realist and minimalist are more recently discovered perspectives. The realist can have the most accurate perspective of the glass of water and look at it for what it is—a glass of water. The realist may not experience an emotional response from the glass of water, which isn't always positive. Their perspective may not have an emotional attachment to the external object. Imagine a life that doesn't inspire or evoke an emotional charge with something external. Our attitude and our feelings shape our interaction with the world. Minimalist perspective looks at the glass of water and says if we keep the glass at mid-point, we can save the additional water for later. The minimalist focuses on making sure basic needs are met first by asking, "Do I need this?" or "What's the least I can get by on?"

It really doesn't matter which perspective you take. Throughout my life and at any given time I can adopt any of these perspectives; what is most important is to identify how they serve you and how they limit your greatness. Your challenge may be to determine why you have a perspective. Where did it come from? More than likely, your past and unresolved relationships or issues are playing out in how you perceive the world. For example, I grew up with few financial resources and moved around a lot. My mother did the best she could to raise my sister and me as the sole provider. At times things were desolate and scarce—there was always just enough. Now, in my adult life, I can perceive my financial situation as "not enough and the ship will sink so I better save more and more." I find myself in this crisis perspective often. With an awareness of how my outlook has been contaminated from the past, I can adjust. For example, I can create a budget and monitor credits and debits or meet with a financial planner to discuss options. I can move through my limited perspective to broaden my scope of vision

Most of the time, I have a whimsical-universe-navigating perspective about things, which is rooted in my family of origin. During my childhood when money and opportunities were scarce, my mother would say "The universe has a plan for us," or "Everything happens for a reason," or "It will all work out." These perspectives have helped me to accept many adversities in my life. My wife is the opposite: her perspective is usually rooted in logic and reason. It's amazing to see how our childhood family dynamics influence our perspectives of ourselves and the world around us. If you are not fond of your attitude and perspective, change it. Sometimes looking through another lens can shift our mindset. For example, I felt frustrated that my wife didn't want to travel from Louisville, Kentucky to Paris, France two months before our child was born. My attitude transformed from free-flowing and accepting to judgmental and bitter. Once I observed the problem from her lens, I attained clarity and demonstrated compassion. If you tend to lean toward a pessimistic perspective, consider looking at the situation through your least favorite lens—maybe as an optimist or a realist. Perspective continues to play an integral role in getting what you deserve from life because it is how you look at everything.

Most often, our attitude shapes our perspective. Anytime I experience a negative attitude towards a new process at work, the perspective that usually follows is, "Here we go. Changing something again. Like *this* shit is going to work." Ninety-nine percent of the time, the outcome is that I am miserable, unhappy and resentful. I get robbed of peace of mind. Negative attitudes skew perspective and steal our happiness. Observe people with negative attitudes and determine if they are truly happy. Whenever I'm feeling negative, I should just say, "I don't really want to be happy today," and admit that my perspective is creating *unhappiness*, even though I want the opposite. Is happiness something you want to maximize while on earth? If it is, I invite you to consider how your attitude may be creating unhappiness in your life.

Having been in recovery for many years, I have learned all the famous phrases. One of my favorites, "Have an attitude of gratitude," has transformed not only my attitude but my perspective on everything. It is hard for me to be grateful and pissed at the same time. When I am grateful, I leave space in my heart for positive things like forgiveness and compassion. Still, I often get frustrated and irritated (ask my wife) but in the long run it doesn't serve me to be in that place. Why? I strive for mental clarity and emotional stability, and an ungrateful attitude fuels destruction. There are many ways to tweak your attitude by adding a smidgen of gratitude. When you find yourself angry, ungrateful, resentful, or discontented, shift your thoughts to the positive things in your life. If it's too challenging for you to do that, think of all the people who are dealing with an even worse situation. Then imagine the kind of world we could experience if everyone felt genuine gratitude and openly shared all their reasons for being grateful with each other.

When I start finding fault with everything about my house and how I can't wait to move, I begin to look at it as a dirty dump – even though it is a cute little house. How can I change my attitude? I can begin to say, "What about all those people who don't have a house or central air or a big-ass TV or...".

There will always be someone somewhere who has it way worse than you. Gratitude is so powerful that it changes brain functioning by releasing the neurotransmitter dopamine, which is associated with pleasure and life-sustaining activity. Your happiness may depend on your level of gratitude! Get over yourself and find gratitude for what you do have. Besides, I was ungrateful for my shoes until I met a man with no feet.

CHAPTER 1 SHIFTS AND MOVEMENTS

- ✗ Ask yourself, "What am I grateful for right now?" Bring at least three things to mind.
- ✗ Now, share your gratitude with someone else and listen to what they are grateful for.
- ✗ Next, take a moment to reflect on those people who have made the biggest impact on your life. As you bring their faces into your awareness and remember the moments you shared with them, say out loud, "Thank you." Envision them receiving your thankfulness and replying, "You're welcome." Allow yourself to feel the gratitude they have been inspiring in you.

ATTITUDE & PERSPECTIVE

EXPRESS GRATITUDE

- ✗ Start your day with gratitude before you get out of bed. This small act can make a profound shift in how you begin your day.

11

x Keep a gratitude journal and place it in a centrally located place in your home or office. Leave it open and encourage others to jot down their daily gratitude in the journal. This will allow you to see what your family or coworkers are grateful for, which can help you develop more gratitude, closeness, and empathy for those whom you love and deeply care for.

x Every night before bed make a small list of five to 10 items for which you are grateful for from that day. It's an excellent practice for reflecting on the day's events and minimizing any negative feelings you may have before you attempt to sleep. Remember, a clear consciousness is the softest pillow.

HAVE AN EMPATHETIC VIEWPOINT

x Empathy is different from sympathy. Empathy is the ability to put yourself in someone else's shoes; sympathy means to pity someone. Try putting yourself in someone else's shoes—literally. Sit down with a friend and swap shoes for a few minutes. Feel the physical sensation of wearing someone else's shoes. It will be an odd experience, but it can stimulate profound conversation and connectedness. Take an even greater risk -- walk a mile in their shoes!

x Next, swap shoes with someone in the metaphorical sense. Listen to their story without saying anything. We all have a story to tell and for the sake of our own healing, it's important to tell it. Try closing your eyes as you listen to their story to see if you can visualize the experience. Note: Let the person know what you are doing so they don't think you are bored and trying to sleep through their whole narrative.

EXPERIENCE A DIFFERENT CULTURE

- If you have the means, travel. Traveling is an excellent way to expose ourselves to the diverse world we live in.
- Talk with people who are different than you to get their perspective. Attend cultural events hosted by your city or town.
- Eat at restaurants that are different than your ethnicity or culture.

ASK QUESTIONS

Ask questions. When you talk with people in your life, spend three-quarters of the conversation asking them questions and listening to their responses instead of sharing your opinions. Listen to understand, not to respond.

ENGAGE IN HEALTHY DEBATE

Engage in a healthy debate with someone in your life - with a catch. You must debate from the other person's opposing viewpoint. Notice how challenging it can be and what feelings and thoughts you experience while debating.

CHAPTER 2

HUMOR. STOP TAKING YOURSELF SERIOUSLY.

"If I had no sense of humor, I would long ago have committed suicide."
MAHATMA GANDHI

I believe appropriate humor is effective medicine for the soul. Nothing compares to a deep belly laugh that makes me cry. Some of the most joyful moments in my life have happened from listening to a baby giggle and laugh – something about it is so innocent, pure, and beautiful. Have you ever laughed because you witnessed someone else laugh? Humor can be contagious. I remember growing up and watching *America's Funniest Home Videos* and laughing at the people who fell and got hurt after taking a bad slip on the ski slope. Yes, I laughed at others' pain and misfortune. That's not a new quality. People have been laughing at others since the beginning of time—it's considered a form of entertainment. The emperors in ancient Rome knew this and capitalized on it by presenting gladiator battles in the coliseum, where people would sustain horrific injuries or even suffer an agonizing death.

Yep, "Hail Emperor, those who are about to die, salute you," the well-known Latin phrase popularized in contemporary society, was reportedly used by captives and criminals whose fate was to die during mock Naval encounters for the pleasure of Emperor Claudius. Puts things in perspective, doesn't it? Can you image dying for the amusement of an assembled crowd? It makes heckling a lousy comedian on stage seem tame by comparison. Even in more civil times, however, some humans still delight in other people's pain, a phenomenon defined by the German word "schadenfreude."

Humor can also be used as a defense mechanism. We use these mostly unconscious defenses to ward off environmental threats. For example, when I get nervous and anxious, I tend to hide behind humor. Growing up, I was the class clown and I mastered the art of humor to hide my true feelings of sadness and terror. I had to laugh to keep from crying.

In recovery circles I've heard people say, "My God has a sense of humor." I say, "The Universe is funny." Both statements mean the same thing. Humor can equal humility, and humility means knowledge of the role I'm assigned in the grand scheme of things. However, being humiliated is *not* funny. Having been humiliated many times in my life, I can tell you there was nothing shit-funny about it. We shouldn't be the butt of anyone's humor. The actual ass is the one laughing at the expense of others. Gossiping about and criticizing others are short-sighted methods people use to inflate their egos and compensate for their own lack of worthiness. Let's be honest: no one likes to experience being "one-down" with another person. Slander and targeting someone's imperfections is an attempt to "right-size" oneself while ignoring the true value of showing compassion and love towards another.

By contrast, the humility I speak of arises from noticing we aren't really a big deal because there are no big deals in life. Humility is about accepting our humanness. Remembering that I am human allows me to understand that I will fail and have difficult times--like all the other humans I share this world with. How often have I wasted time because I took myself too seriously? Try not taking yourself, your job, or your homework too seriously and notice what comes up for you. You may find that your heart opens to the possibilities and gifts life offers. Through humor, we can experience our soft and amusing existence. Or, *bah humbug!* We can choose humor and humility or Scrooge and bitterness.

My first job out of graduate school was at a mental health organization, a non-profit that accepted clients on Medicaid. The treatment center featured the typical stereotypes—groups were crowded, caseloads were high, and the clients' substance use was chronic and severe. It didn't take much to feel overwhelmed. There I was, fresh out of school and trying to make a name for myself. Jim, my supervisor at the time, was a very spiritual man who always had a smile on his face and a funny joke to tell. He was the type of leader who rolled with the punches and took whatever came down the pike. One day during supervision, I was processing a case or complaining about my caseload when he stopped me and said, "Don't forget to breathe." There it was. The key to life: breath—literally.

Sometimes taking things too seriously can lead to being overwhelmed with stress. The brain, when stressed, secretes hormones such as cortisol that is interpreted as a threat. In this threatening downward spiral, stress leads to poor decision-making, emotional overreactions, and an increased likelihood of mental, emotional and physical health issues. Intentional breathing calms the autonomic nervous system (ANS) and regulates and restores our bodies to a state of balance so we can function optimally. When you feel yourself becoming too serious, stop. And don't forget to breathe.

CHAPTER 2 SHIFTS AND MOVEMENTS

What makes me human?

_____

_____

_____

How do I allow myself to have fun?

_____

_____

_____

Do I need to create more fun in my life? How?

_____

_____

_____

When was a time I experienced humiliation?

_____

_____

_____

What happened? Who was there?

_____

_____

_____

How did I overcome that experience?

_____

_____

_____

What does humility mean to me?

_____

_____

_____

How have I practiced humility in my life?

_____

_____

_____

How can I practice humility more often?

_____

_____

_____

Take a break from reading for a moment. Now, focus on laughing. Allow yourself to awkwardly laugh and continue to laugh until it feels natural. Try exaggerating your laugh to make the experience more intense. How was that? Refreshing, huh?

Smile. Stop what you're doing right now and smile. Smile so big that it feels awkward. Hold the smile for a few seconds and relax your face. What do you notice in your mood and thoughts at this very moment?

MAKE HUMOR AND LAUGHTER A PART OF YOUR LIFE

Find ways to laugh, as in a deep-belly-tears-in-eyes kind of laughter. Here are a few ways to do it:

- x Google videos of babies laughing and watch it. You will enjoy it.
- x Look up corny jokes and tell them to your coworkers and colleagues.
- x Write your own corny jokes.
- x During your daily routine, be sure to laugh at something silly or annoying that happens.

Remember, You're Not That Important (Even Though You Are)

Instead of taking yourself so seriously, find humor in stiff and rigid thinking.

- x Allow yourself to feel natural feelings and body sensations through journaling and other creative writing processes.
- x Dance. I mean anywhere. If you're at a department store and a funky song comes on, stop what you are doing and dance. It is goofy; everyone will probably stare at you, but most importantly you will laugh.
- x Sing in the shower.
- x Go to a toy store and walk around. What do you notice in the environment? What do you notice within yourself?
- x Begin a yoga practice. Yoga has many physical, mental and emotional health benefits and developing a yoga

practice may help you access the playful and vulnerable part of yourself.

x Purchase or rent your favorite childhood books. After reading them, notice what feelings and memories are present. What values, metaphors and meaning do you take away from these books?

Draw a picture of your favorite toy as a child.

When I look at the picture of the toy I feel:

_____

_____

_____

When I look at the picture of the toy I think:

_____

_____

_____

What makes this toy special?

_____

_____

_____

What memories do I have in my life related to this toy?

_____

_____

_____

Do I allow myself to play and be childlike?

_____

_____

_____

If not, what age did I give myself permission to not play and be childlike?

_____

_____

_____

What are ways I can be playful now?

_____

_____

_____

CHAPTER 3:

LOVE: MOVING BEYOND CUPID

"Love is our true destiny. We do not find the meaning of life by ourselves alone - we find it with another."

THOMAS MERTON

Love is not a feeling or emotion. Love is not a term of endearment. Love can be a state of being. Love is an action so profound it can change the course of humanity. Love is a selfless act to demonstrate affection to something external (or internal when we love ourselves). Love is powerful. Love creates space for curiosity, openness and acceptance— and these attributes can also help us move closer to love. When I practice curiosity, openness to myself and others, and acceptance, sometimes the result is experiencing love. When a baby is born and finally held by its mother, that's love. The most intense love I've ever experienced was the day my daughter, Elliette, was born. I continue to experience unconditional love because of her! Neuroscience has concluded that something magically happens during that intimate moment between mother and baby— secure attachment. The baby's brain produces oxytocin, a neurotransmitter that lets baby know that Momma is safe and can be trusted. That is the ultimate loving bond. Our brains never stop producing oxytocin. In fact, when you walk into work or a recovery meeting and a friend gives you a hug and you feel safe and secure—that's oxytocin.

It appears that during this technological wave of history, characterized by globalization and quick internet access, we are more connected. However, as humans, the connections we crave go far beyond our keyboards and Wi-Fi signals. We desire true human connection. We crave physical touch. Sometimes when I am anxious and overwhelmed with deadlines, a simple hand on my shoulder or back grounds me. Witnessing people close to me struggle with sex addiction led me to this conclusion: the addiction is a result of touch deprivation. We will find what we need in healthy or self-destructive ways. Although human touch has lost its popularity, when healthy touch is reintroduced into our relationships, healing properties are available. Touch can activate calming sensations when we experience states of frustration and disturbance.

In 1938, at Harvard University, a longitudinal study began that is still being researched through data collection from the original study groups. This 80-year study sought to reveal what makes humans the happiest. It wasn't the amount of income or investments, the size of the house the participants lived in, or the career choice that led to happiness. The study concluded that the quality of our relationships is what makes us happiest. We are hard-wired to want and need love, connection, and support. We will find a way to get them, whether healthy or unhealthy. Addictions are an attempt to make attachment so that our most basic desires and needs are met. Erich Fromm, in *The Art of Loving* describes the theory of love as, "love, the answer to the problem of human existence." Think about the problems you may have in your life. Could love be a solution? I think of all the strained relationships I've had in the past: the antidote was love. Every time I get frustrated, love is the answer. Love involves compassion and understanding, which is no small feat.

Love is reciprocal between personal and interpersonal relationships. The love dilemma is, to love or be loved. Most of us struggle with one of these concepts. For me, to give love is easier. I will give all my love until I have none for myself. Ask yourself, "Is it more challenging for me to love or be loved?" Receiving self-love and love from others can pose a formidable challenge for many reasons. Maybe you don't feel worthy of love? If you never had someone model healthy love throughout your life, it can seem impossible to be open for love. If you have a tough time showing yourself love, it may be almost impossible to let others love you. People who hold underlying negative beliefs like "I am unlovable," "I am undeserving," or "I am unworthy," adopted them at any early age and they were reinforced throughout their life. We will look for things in the world and in our relationships that reinforce what we believe about ourselves.

When at the edge of receiving love, these beliefs can manifest as a noticeably subtle resistance. For example, when my wife and I were dating, I always felt a knot it my stomach when I said, "I love you." Upon closer examination, I realized that I was saying "I love you" without believing it in return. It was painful to hear those three words because I believed I was unlovable. *Besides, how could she love me with all the shit I've done? And, because I am unlovable, why would she stay with me? She will leave me, like every other woman in my life, going all the way back to my mother.* Well, my wife is still here, and I found out that I am lovable. In fact, I recently texted her, "Thank you for loving me," and within minutes her response was "Thank you for allowing me to love you." Will we "allow" people to love us? Who do you struggle to let love you?

We all have these internal scripts that determine our level of self-love and love from others. First, I had to become conscious to what my experience and sensations were telling me. A newfound consciousness led me to curiosity. Once curious, I could track the internal messages. The messages always lead me to the pot of gold. Most of these internal dialogues are inaccurate due to the fact of our perception at the time of the initial experience. When we revisit the past from a fresh perspective, we can see things differently. When analyzing our past, it's not about what really happened, it's what sense we make of the past—the meaning we give it. I found out that my mom didn't leave me because I was unlovable. It was just the opposite: she sent my sister and me to live with my father because that was the best solution for our well-being and hers under the circumstances. She needed a break to figure her life out. My mother has been and will continue to be the love of my life and my greatest teacher. I love you Mom!

In recovery they say, "Let us love you until you can learn to love yourself." You are the common denominator and most important person in your life. You deserve your love more than anybody in your life and sometimes we need to see in ourselves what others see. At some point, though, our self-love is our responsibility. When I think of how I love myself, two words come to mind: grace and mercy. Grace allows me to honor myself for who I am at this exact moment without expectations. Mercy delivers compassion and forgiveness to us or to someone else. When I find it difficult to meet a specific goal, I can put the whip down and be gentle with myself for the diligent work I've done up to that point. So, how can you demonstrate love to those people in your life? Is grace and mercy a foreign language you wish you could speak? Remember to take care of yourself and nurture your soul with love. Embracing love can lead to abundant joy and happiness!

CHAPTER 3 SHIFTS AND MOVEMENTS

Pause here. Wrap both arms around yourself and give yourself a big hug. Close your eyes and feel the embrace. With your arms crossed in the hugging position, begin to gently caress your biceps and forearms. Keep breathing deeply while rubbing your arms for 1-2 minutes. Notice what that feels like. Record the experience here:

_____

_____

_____

_____

_____

What does *love* mean to me?

_____

_____

_____

Who taught me the meaning of *love*?

_____

_____

_____

How do I show others I *love* them?

_____

_____

_____

Are there any obstacles for allowing others to *love* me?

_____

_____

_____

What is the greatest *love* I have ever experienced?

_____

_____

_____

How does love feel?

_____

_____

_____

What holds me back from experiencing love from others?

_____

_____

_____

When I think of love I think of these images, experiences or memories:

_____

_____

_____

Feel in the blank: I love myself because _____

_____!

(write this on a notecard or post-it note and place it where it can be seen throughout the day or week.)

I love _____

because _____!

(now share this with that person)

THE GREATEST GIFT YOU CAN GIVE TO OTHERS

Write someone a love letter in your life. Hide it somewhere that they are likely to find it. For example, sometimes I hide notes in my wife's lunch so she can find it when she eats. She is always surprised, and it lets her know how much I appreciate her. Before I leave town for business trips, I will usually write her a letter or poem and leave it for her to find when she gets home.

- x If you love someone, then tell them. You better mean it though.
- x Perform acts of kindness for people in your life and complete strangers too.

× Experiment: When hugging someone, preferably someone you know, allow yourself to hug for several minutes. This is an effective way to connect with others and allows the brain to release oxytocin.

THE GREATEST GIFT YOU CAN GIVE YOURSELF

× Write yourself a love letter and put it away somewhere safe. Monthly, annually or whenever you need a lift, pull out the letter and read it to yourself.
× Create a mantra or affirmation and review it daily. Say it out loud to yourself.
× Treat yourself to something nice (you're worth it).
× Let others tell you they love you.
× Let others perform acts of kindness for you.
× Be gentle and have mercy on yourself.
× Engage in self-care. Finding ways to debrief and take care of emotional and mental stress is important to prevent exhaustion.

CHAPTER 4:

PASSION: HARNESSING AMBITION THROUGH ACTION

"Passion is the genesis of genius."
TONY ROBBINS

Love and passion are two different experiences. Love can be a loaded word with many different meanings. When most people think of love, their minds tend to gravitate toward sex, chocolates, romance...and maybe even popcorn. I think we can probably all agree that sex is awesome. However, it is one tiny facet of the love pool. If that's true, then what is passion? Can we create an internal loving mechanism that harnesses our passion? Certainly, both love and passion have gotten me in trouble in my life, but I have learned through experience to let love direct my passion while remaining grounded in my morals. You can too. And in case you're wondering, my newfound passion was not boring; far from it. Rather than fizzling out in a firecracker of unsustainable emotion, my love-directed passion gave me the foundation I needed to thrive.

Let me put it another way: have you ever felt passionate about some new idea or trend, only to have your intensity vaporize as quickly as it appeared? Maybe you talked yourself out of it or caved to other people's negative opinions about it. Either way, think about how you handled the outcome. Did you get frustrated, throw your arms up in the air, and proclaim, "The hell with it anyways?" Did you deny yourself greatness because you lost your juice? I've been meaning to write this book for many years. When I first finished graduate school, I didn't know who I was and what to do with my time. That's when I began writing some of the ideas for this book. However, I wasn't very passionate about it. I stayed busy to avoid the feelings of grief and loss that resulted from the void I'd created by completing a tremendous task -- graduating. I never wrote the book until now.

Maybe I needed more experience? Maybe I wasn't ready to direct my thoughts towards something inspiring? Who fucking knows honestly? I do know that I lost my mojo, my passion. Recently something stirred up in my soul and inspired me to put fingers to keyboard. This book's physical creation has manifested many opportunities. I have had some intense conversations with people about life and their experiences. The titles of the chapters have been like headings in different scenarios in my common day-to-day grind. I have been seeing this book live out in my life. And I fucking hate writing.

I recently had a conversation with my friend and hip-hop artist Dolla Green, a.k.a. Rickey Green, and he gave me a great description of passion. He said, "The translation of passion means to suffer. For example, I am passionate about being a father and there is suffering in that [anxiety, lack of sleep, and the selfless act of thinking of others]. One who is passionate about working out suffers for it." I must agree that everything I've been passionate about has led to suffering. But why? Why must we suffer and experience pain with passion?

Passion led Romeo to kill himself in *Romeo and Juliet*. When not harnessed, passion has the power to kill. I have treated many people suffering from substance use disorder. These populations take suffering to an extreme and experience much passion along the way. I'm usually amazed at how creative and intelligent my clients are. I have treated everything from musicians, Golden Glove boxers, aspiring artists—you name it. For them, there is an inflated cost to their passion.

The beginning of our greatness is passion. Passion is motivation before motivation is harnessed. Passion must be at the core of your personal movement towards developing into the person you want to be. Our ambitions drive us to be better, more thoughtful, and more loving...and that starts with suffering. What are you willing to suffer for? In *The Passion of Christ*, Jesus suffered for humanity and ultimately resurrected and overcame suffering. Suffering is only temporary. In *The Alchemist,* Paulo Coelho eloquently states that "fear of suffering is more painful than suffering itself." Thoughts, ideas, and concepts do not change our lives or the world around us, nor do they heal our suffering. Thoughts can vanish just as quickly as they arrive; however, directing our thoughts and feelings with action is where passion is bred. When the intensity of passion increases, we want to "strike while the iron is hot." Acting and tapping into this ambition can create a multitude of personal and interpersonal opportunities that can increase passion and direction. The more passion you have, the more suffering you experience. If you seek passion, be ready to suffer.

When untamed, passion is dangerous, much like the image of the Mad Scientist who stays locked in the laboratory creating monsters. Adolf Hitler was extremely passionate. Don't believe me? Watch one of his speeches. However, we know how it ended: with the murders of tens of millions of innocent humans, mostly Jewish, throughout Europe. Misdirected passion causes chaos and destruction.

Passion is not enough. Passion is the soil from which the flowers of your garden will grow. Flowers need many different elements other than soil, but soil is the foundation. Your mission starts with passion. What moves you? What really gets you juiced up? Once you identify that passion, you can strategize and create plans to make your passion come to fruition and, like Christ, you can experience your own resurrection. You must suffer first, though. Passion in our lives is important--we need something that we can wake up to in the morning and something to live for.

CHAPTER 4 SHIFTS AND MOVEMENTS

Reflect on your life, review what has made you passionate, and record your answers here:

_____

_____

_____

What does passion mean to me?

_____

_____

_____

What am I passionate about now?

_____

_____

_____

How has being passionate led to suffering?

_____

_____

_____

How did I overcome my suffering?

_____

_____

_____

What stories, myths, and fairy tales about passion resonate
with me?

_____

_____

_____

Was there suffering in these stories?

_____

_____

_____

Who suffered and how?

_____

_____

_____

How do these sufferings relate to my own sufferings?

_____

_____

_____

What have I always wanted to try or explore for the first time?

_____

_____

_____

Who do I know that I see as being passionate about something?

_____

_____

_____

How can they help me focus on my passion?

_____

_____

_____

Now reach out to that person and share your passion!

PASSION IS CONTAGIOUS

- x Talk with others about their passions. Notice how intense the conversation can get when multiple people share what they're passionate about.
- x Talk to others about how they have failed and suffered as related to their passions.
- x Do something that you're curious about -- sign up for a cooking class, buy art supplies and create something, or take swim lessons.

- Activate your childlike mindset; be playful, spontaneous, and creative. Let your mind wander about the possibilities and be in a state of "awe" over the world you live in.
- Be curious and examine the resources available to you that could ignite your passion and inspire your greatness.

CHAPTER 5

ADVENTURE AND RISK: SEEKING REWARDS

"The biggest adventure you can take is to live the life of your dreams."

OPRAH WINFREY

We have become comfortable in our current technological state where everything is within arm's reach. Yet we've lost our ability to be spontaneous and take bold steps toward jeopardy because we have become complacent and stagnated on our couches and smartphones. The ancient rumbling in our souls that gets stirred up by contemplating possibilities is dissipating. We are no longer self-guiding but led by television and social media advertisements, new reality TV drama (which isn't an accurate perception of reality), and our political spearheads. Somehow our culture has adopted this mentality of, "Netflix and chill." Don't get me wrong; I enjoy all these things, which have made life more comfortable. But something happens to me when I deny myself primordial pleasure. I get lost within a seven-foot range between my television and couch while my soul slowly evaporates into my flesh until I become nothing more than a shell...a fucking lifeless machine.

We have lost our sense of adventure within our culture. We have substituted complacency for authentic, unusual life experiences that enrich us and disrupt the monotony of life. We have become quite routine and efficient in the way we choose to live, avoiding healthy risk and reward. Why is this a problem? Because of the way we're wired, such avoidance can compel us to take unhealthy risks with high rewards including technology and substance addiction, overeating, and extramarital affairs.

A part of us craves adventure and excitement and wants to pioneer *something*. Up to this point in the book, I've shared some simple and effective tools to get the ball rolling. Our soul's cauldron brews these concepts of love, attitude, perspective, humor and passion. So now what? Do you want to stop here? Is this good enough or do you want more? You are standing at the brink of adventure in your life. What happens next? Adventure. What do you need to do to get to where you want to be? What's your move? Wait a minute, though. Once you embark on your life's adventure, nothing will be the same. Your couch will never feel the same. Your habits and obsessions may never feel quite as good as they did before. The news, social media, and other technology outlets may not be as seductive. The old life that has become tiring will never be the same. And the shell of a person you've become? It will die and be replaced a new, vibrant being with a fresh perspective on the world.

Over the years I've worked with clients in my private practice that have reported being "stuck" in their life. I have observed these clients as they drew shallow breaths and withered away in a slow, painful death resulting from not pursuing their adventure. Every individual's adventure is unique. For some it could involve moving across the state to attend college; for others, starting a new tech business or becoming parents for the first time. No matter how you define it, pursuing your true adventure requires risk. For the many clients I've worked with in the past who were not getting the big payoff from life (reward), it was their unwillingness to take a risk that was to blame. The reward reflects the risk; low-risk equals low-reward.

Imagine, you are standing at the threshold of your adventure. You can see out into the distance some outcome or result. You try to take a step forward, but you do not budge. Your wildest dreams are within your eye's view, yet you cannot move. As you watch this adventure fade away into nothingness, your passion for conquering something new subsides. The result? You're alone with no vision, nothing to look at or aspire to. What's that like for you? Did you notice the resistance?

The greatest risk ever taken was not taking a risk at all. Without risk-taking, you are stuck – and you will remain stuck until you decide to move. Risk-taking is not popular; it can also pose a challenging task to the over-analytical thinker who does a "checks-and-balances" to determine if the risk is rewarding enough. This person becomes indecisive, refuses to budge, and becomes stuck with ideas while trying to figure out the endgame. The passive and withdrawn person may quiver at the idea of taking risks and will procrastinate to avoid the uncomfortable feelings that come with them. This type ultimately becomes avoidant and experiences despair and depression as they sink into a hole of their own creation.

The people-pleaser will gauge risk-taking as it relates to others and will only take risks to win approval, which in the end is short-lived. This type of risk-taker ends up losing both battles--pleasing others and feeling pleased with oneself. Because the actual risk is getting approval from others and not the risk for oneself, then they find themselves in a check-mate situation until they can learn to make decisions and take risks for their own happiness. Taking risks for others' happiness leads to unhappiness. The compulsive risk-taker will take uncalculated risks, fail to learn from errors, and continue to take short-gain risks with high intensity. This person is thrill-seeking; the risk isn't about a meaningful outcome, but rather the feeling and intense sensations that come with the short gain.

I have traveled all over the world and walked across Sydney Harbor Bridge in Sydney, Australia. I have stood atop Mount Stanserhorn in the Swiss Alps, Switzerland. I have flown all over the world and have traveled to many heights. I have experienced roller coasters of all sizes, sat on the edge of cliffs, and parasailed in Daytona, Florida.

In August of 2016, as best man in my best friend's wedding, I helped coordinate a weekend getaway to Red River Gorge (RRG) in the backwoods of Kentucky – a scenic place with picturesque views at every turn of the head. Having never been to RRG before, I was excited. Some of the dudes who were going had been there before and they mentioned going cliff jumping that Saturday. I was just as hyped as everyone else and looked forward to taking a risk. Saturday came and we hiked along a river, until the trees opened to reveal a huge flat rock wavering above the water. We had arrived on time because people were already jumping off the cliff into the water. Our crew started taking our shirts off and trash-talking each other. Most of us waded through the water to the riverbank so we could climb the rock to jump.

I stood across the rock and watched these men, my friends, jump roughly 20 feet into the river. It looked invigorating and I had every intention of following their example. About that time, they started shouting my name, which really juiced me up. I made my climb atop the rock, walked to the edge, looked out at everyone (at least 30 people), and shifted my focus to the water. Then, I shifted my focus to the crowd and back to the water in a recurring pattern I repeated several times. People started to cheer for me to jump, while my friends all stood around and gave me words of encouragement. However, I froze. I did not jump. I was scared. My heart rate was through the roof. I decided to sit down on that rock where everyone was hanging out. Every time I stood up and looked at the edge I shook, consumed with fear and shame. I blasted myself with tons of negative self-talk and experienced the regrettable feeling of being "less than." For crying out loud, *little children* were jumping off this cliff. If my friend's dog Bella could have gotten up there, I'm sure she would have jumped. I was mortified.

The shame of that moment stayed with me the rest of that afternoon and all night. The following day, Sunday, most of the guys left the cabin to return to their families, but about six of us stayed and hiked back to the cliff. This was it. I was going to jump this time. I spent all day hyping myself up and preparing to jump. *I will be redeemed! This is my chance to prove to everyone that I am a man (whatever that means)!* We got to the tree openings and I saw the cliff. I began to slosh through the murky water, climbed to it, then walked to the edge of the cliff and, with all the determination and courage I could muster...froze. *What the fuck.* I couldn't move. Again? What is this? I hung out on the rock and every so often, walked to the edge to peer over. I finally got to a place of "I'm not going to do it, and I'm okay with that." That was it. That was my self-permission statement that let me off the hook.

This story is a metaphor for adventure and risk in our real lives. We get to the edge of adventure – the place where only a burning desire to take that specific risk can compel us to follow through – and shut down physically, mentally, emotionally and spiritually. We talk about how this time it is going to be different. Guess what? It's the same. Nothing changes if nothing changes. How many times have you been on the edge with the people in your life cheering and rooting for you to take the next step, and you either freeze or head off in the opposite direction of your adventure? The crowd is waiting to see your greatness and you shrink. I didn't take the risk – not because I'm scared of heights but because I would not have had control. Plus, it was comfortable and warm sitting on my rock. Risk, by definition, is uncomfortable and uncertain. If it's predictable and comfortable, it's not a risk.

In my example, every time I stood up, some people cheered, and I sat down again. We tell people about a new adventure we are set on and they give us a positive affirmation, then we sit back down in our shame of not being good enough. I understand that's a generalized statement, but you have your internal dialogue that minimizes the risk you take by sending you messages. Not true? If it wasn't true, you'd be an astronaut or a prime minister somewhere. You would have followed your dreams and taken the risks to get the reward.

The biggest adventure I've ever been on has been my recovery from substance use disorder. My lineage has been plagued with addictive genetics: from my father on down, the men in my family have suffered from mental health and severe substance use disorder. These were good men who farmed and fought in wars to protect their country but were rattled by internal torture and anguish. When I was just five years old, my grandfather, Shirley, committed suicide. I thought that's the way it was supposed to be. Until I turned 24 years-old, their truth was my truth. Later I realized that my grandfather, a World War II veteran and hero, who was adorned with numerous medals including the Purple Heart for his bravery at war, suffered tremendously with little relief until he eventually found *his* relief. He did the very best he could with the resources he had. When I got sober and realized addiction was a highway to nowhere, people in my life questioned my choice to go to rehab. Now most of them are either dead or incarcerated, or on their way to being dead or incarcerated. I can hear and feel Shirley behind me, cheering and rooting for my accomplishments. Without him, I have no father and there is no me. I'm grateful for that.

By the time I was 16, I was strung out on methamphetamines and multiple substances. I used marijuana daily and prided myself on being a "pothead." I was the ultimate stoner and burnout. The first time I took a pain pill (an opiate base, like heroin) I fell in love and chased that feeling for many years. Before I got sober, I was spending $300 daily on OxyContin (not counting the money I spent daily on booze and weed). But something shifted one morning when I woke up and heard the birds chirping. It was not a new experience, yet somehow it was different. The birds sounded happy and vibrant. Whereas most mornings, I heard a hellish squaw that prevented me from sleeping or enjoying my high, this time I heard a pleasing melody. Most nights I would use a cocktail of substances to help me "sleep." If I woke up in the middle of the night, I'd use something to help me fall back to sleep. At that moment, I wasn't using to get intoxicated, but to feel and appear normal and avoid withdrawal symptoms and many years of trauma and emotional pain.

That morning, I thought to myself, "I'm going to go to rehab." Well, I did fulfill my commitment...three months later. Addiction is powerful. I wanted to stop, but I could not, even though every day I vowed, "This is it. I'm going to change." And every day I repeated the same destructive behavior until I was in enough emotional and spiritual pain to take the risk. This was probably the first time I coherently stood at the edge of the cliff: the pain of staying the same felt worse than the pain of changing. At 24, I didn't know what I didn't know. I was young, naïve, and thought the world owed me something. I knew something had to be better; I just didn't know what that was. I hoped that if I took the adventure, I would get the reward and I didn't know what that would be. And my hopes were fulfilled because the rewards have been abundant! Early in that adventure, however, I thought it was a waste of time and that the rewards weren't coming fast enough. What if the greatest explorers and inventors gave up halfway into their adventure? The reward would not have been achieved to its fullest potential or at all. Don't give up before the miracle happens! Don't stop before you get what you deserve. My struggle with drug addiction is the same experience as someone struggling with an eating disorder or grappling with the decision to leave a toxic relationship. The point is, we all have things that block us from fully embracing who want to be and who we are. Claim what's yours! You will have to take the adventure though, and that may require hope and faith.

Your adventure could be a lifetime endeavor of switching careers or planning a big trip. The truth is, the biggest adventure we get is today – the next critical 24 hours ahead of us. If you're willing to accept the challenge, every day can bring excitement and adventure. Ask yourself: *What am I going to accomplish today? What mountain am I going to climb?* Understand, the mountain doesn't care whether you follow through or not; it will still be there after you leave. The adventure of today is the only one we will get, so make it count. Get ready, because you're the only one who can climb and navigate through your challenges. As my personal trainer once said, "The regret of staying in bed is always more painful that the regret of getting to the gym." Will you choose regret or the feelings of triumph?

There is a sense of personal responsibility and dignity associated with risk-taking. It's called a risk for a reason -- it's an exposure to danger -- and there is some level of uncertainty involved; however, creating a plan and being accountable to others in your life can make taking risks less threatening. Getting support and feedback from those who care can increase your opportunity to pursue healthy risks towards getting the most from your life.

CHAPTER 5 SHIFTS AND MOVEMENTS

Examine the risks that you've taken throughout your life.

_____

_____

_____

What risks did I take that led to this moment in my life?

_____

_____

_____

What risks did I avoid?

_____

_____

_____

How would life be different if I took those risks I avoided?

_____

_____

_____

What was my greatest dream/wish as a child?

_____

_____

_____

Did my dream/wish change?

_____

_____

_____

How did my dream/wish change?

_____

_____

_____

What is my greatest dream/wish for myself now? Make a list of your dreams and aspirations.

_____

_____

_____

What are the risks that are limiting my ability to obtain my dreams?

_____

_____

_____

What am I doing to work towards my dream/wish?

_____

_____

_____

What are the foreseeable obstacles that could impact my dream/wish?

_____

_____

_____

When I obtain my dream/wish, how will I feel?

_____

_____

_____

When I obtain my dream/wish, what will I think of myself?

_____

_____

_____

When I obtain my dream/wish, what will I think of others?

_____

_____

_____

ADVENTURE & RISK

x Take a walk in the woods or a park. Look at your surroundings. What do you notice? What sensations are you experiencing?

x Read and watch "adventurous" books and movies. What characters do you relate to? Why?

x Write your own fiction or nonfiction adventure.

x Say "yes" to risk in your life.

CHAPTER 6

HELPING OTHERS: IT'S WHAT WE'RE HERE FOR.

"Everything good that's ever happened to me came out of helping others."
DANNY TREJO

Recovery has taught me one very important thing—help someone else. Helping others is what we're here to do. Our culture is self-consuming and teaches us the opposite: to be independent and get shit done on our own, even though our purpose is to coexist with others and be interdependent. We are often overwhelmed with our own needs and stressors. If we could only fix this or buy that one thing, then we would find happiness. Chapter 3 mentions that connection with others creates the most happiness for humans. What are we connected to though? What binds us as a species? Connection is the gateway for helping, and service to others strengthens that connection. What makes us feel the best in our relationships? When we help others, it makes us feels great. Veronica Ray, author of *I can make a Difference*, states, "There are many ways in which helping others can be a joy. There are ways of finding honor and pride in serving other people and our communities. These positive feelings result from believing we are involved in something greater than ourselves."

It does feel good because providing help to others gives us a feeling of accomplishment for that contribution. Neuroscientists have discovered that dopamine, a neurotransmitter associated with pleasure, is released when we connect to and help others. If you've ever helped someone else in their time of need or been the recipient of help when you needed it, then you know how much joy and gratitude the experience can create. I think the goal is to be of service when we can and when we do that, we find ourselves living enriched lives.

I'm reminded of the story about a man's dream in which he traveled to heaven and hell. First, he went to hell and observed everyone sitting at a banquet table laden with tons of delicious food. They all had enormous forks and spoons tied to their hands, which prevented them from lifting the food to their mouths, and everyone starved. The man was terrified. Next, he went to heaven and discovered a similar scene of everyone sitting at a banquet table laden with tons of delicious food. As in hell, these folks had enormous forks and spoons tied to their hands. However, to the man's amazement, no one starved because they used their utensils to feed each other.

This story illustrates the essence of humanity and offers a sharp contrast to the state of our modern-day connectedness with our community and the world around us. We are distracted from each other with our self-consumed ways and lifestyle. The antidote to self-absorption and loneliness is connection; the ability to contribute to another person's life cycle in a subtle or profound manner. When we think of others – something we were created to do – we lose focus on our own menial problems and frustrations. Keep in mind, it doesn't have to involve heroics. Helping someone may simply mean holding the door open; making a phone call to a friend because you know they are struggling; or sitting with a family member during a crisis. The Dalai Lama states, "Our prime purpose in this life is to help others. And if you can't help them, at least don't hurt them."

Helping others creates opportunities for the universe to show us its magic. Several years ago, we received an absurd amount of snow in Kentucky—six inches, enough to shut down the entire city of Louisville and many surrounding counties. My wife and I had just moved into our house that previous August. Our neighbors were a very sweet and generous elderly couple who both had physical health issues. I got my snow shovel from my shed and proceeded to clean my driveway and sidewalk. After I finished my area, I walked to my neighbors and shoveled their sidewalk, driveway, vehicles, and the little space where Chuck enjoyed his cigarettes. To me this was no big deal; I was doing what I thought any human could do. I imagined myself and Elise being elderly in this kind of weather and hoped that someone would help us. As I was finishing up, Chuck came to his cigarette spot to thank me, grateful that they could leave to go to the store. I shook his hand and told him that's what neighbors are for.

My yard isn't that big but using a handheld push mower can get frustrating and difficult in the humid Kentucky summer heat. I came home one day from work and noticed my front lawn had been mowed. As I walked to my backyard, I noticed Chuck riding his big John Deere tractor, grinning from ear to ear. After he finished, I thanked him. His response? "I don't mind, and that's what neighbors are for."

Chuck wanted to help me, and he did. He knew what I needed and did the best he could to meet me where I was. That was true for my experience helping Chuck. It felt incredible for both of us. Those two brief moments of helping each other brought closeness to our relationship. Chuck and his wife have since moved to Texas, where they no longer worry about snow removal, but I will never forget the awe I experienced helping a fellow human.

CHAPTER 6 SHIFTS AND MOVEMENTS

Who can I help in my life?

_____

_____

_____

How will I help them?

_____

_____

_____

When will I help them?

_____

_____

_____

What did I think and feel, sometime in the past, when I was able to help someone?

_____

_____

_____

What do I need help with?

_____

_____

_____

Who had the greatest influence on my life?

_____

_____

_____

How did they impact my life?

_____

_____

_____

What values or gifts did they give me?

_____

_____

_____

How have I carried their legacy with me?

_____

_____

_____

Who will I let help me?

_____

_____

_____

How can others help me?

_____

_____

_____

What did I think and feel, sometime in the past, when I was able to let someone help me with a problem or issue?

_____

_____

_____

What are my limitations to helping someone else? (i.e. time, money)

_____

_____

_____

What changes need to occur to shift my limitations for helping others?

_____

_____

_____

Has helping others been a negative experience? How so?

_____

_____

_____

What benefits have I experienced by helping others?

_____

_____

_____

What ways can I support and help your neighbors and people in my community?

_____

_____

_____

How can I help and support colleagues, coworkers or staff?

_____

_____

_____

LENDING A HELPING HAND

- Help somebody and don't tell anyone. Keep your "act of service" to yourself and notice how that feels.
- Volunteer somewhere that interests you as a way of helping humanity.
- Spend five minutes picking up litter in a parking lot or in your neighborhood.

x Engage with people you barely know more often. We never know when someone needs us to check on them. Sometimes it only takes a small conversation to lift someone's mood. Remember, it's not always about you and what is convenient and comfortable. Helping others may involve sacrifice.

CHAPTER 7

PURPOSE AND MEANING: CATAPULTING INTO GREATNESS

"Every great dream begins with a dreamer. Always remember, you have within you the strength, the patience, and the passion to reach for the stars to change the world."
HARRIET TUBMAN

This book has offered some excellent concepts of application that can help launch you into the realm of change. Knowledge is not power: the application of knowledge gives us power. Shifting our perspective and harnessing our passion can lead to an unstoppable and truthful momentum. When aimed in the right direction, this momentum can catapult you into a new existence. Yes, you can choose the direction of your life. You can create your own reality. The challenging part is uncovering or -- possibly for the first time -- *discovering* your purpose and meaning.

> *"Efforts and courage are not enough without purpose and direction."*
> JOHN F. KENNEDY

The last chapter holds a lot of truth about how helping others can create purpose in our lives. I bet you didn't get this book to learn how to become a saint or a priest. You are probably stuck and bored with your mundane life, and you're looking for some spice to mix it up a little bit. You know in your soul that something else is out there for you. You are chasing your calling, your purpose. What is a life worth living if you've never truly lived a life in your day? Our days are numbered. Sometimes the struggle can be the dilemma between knowing our purpose and finding our meaning.

Viktor Frankl, author of *Man's Search for Meaning,* gives us great insight about purpose and meaning. Dr. Frankl was a Jewish psychiatrist who was imprisoned in the Auschwitz concentration camp in Europe during World War II. The amazing thing is that Dr. Frankl was one in 20 survivors during the Holocaust. The harsh environmental conditions that these innocent humans were exposed to, coupled with the physical abuse, made survival almost impossible. Imagine being out in an open field digging holes with broken tools in minus-zero-degree weather, with no shoes and minimal clothing. Imagine being starved, going back to the camp, and only receiving a 750 – to – 1,000 calorie diet daily. Imagine sleeping under dead bodies to keep your body temperature warm. Such horrific experiences are not too far back in our past. Last year, Elise and I traveled to Poland, where we had the humbling opportunity to explore Auschwitz. It was one of the most indescribable experiences of my life. Every tourist looked like they were grieving (which we all were), with their frowns and lifeless facial expressions. Even after visiting, I still can't fathom the magnitude of suffering at Auschwitz. My stomach churned the entire time we were there. I looked at my wife and remarked, "My stomach hurts," and she replied, "Mine too." The trauma and grief were so profound we felt it in our guts. For those who lived through the terror, what did they grasp to help them survive?

Let's explore meaning. Searching for our personal meaning is our primary focus. Like one of Buddhism's core beliefs, Frankl highlights that there is meaning in suffering if we can stay with the pain. What does it mean to suffer? What is your suffering? Is your suffering in vain? Your suffering is yours. It doesn't have to be as far down the scale that some of us have experienced. Your suffering is yours to define. It could be anything that causes emotional, spiritual, physical, and mental pain: the loss of a loved one, being terminated from an employer, struggling to overcome a gambling addiction—these are all forms of suffering. The key is to find meaning. When we find meaning in our suffering, it lessens the pain we experience because the experience becomes about the meaning. To suffer means to fully live life. Through the human birthing process, we come into the world suffering. We are created to suffer, which means we are created to find meaning.

This is difficult because most of us have low thresholds for pain—I know I do. The moment I feel pain I try to find an escape route—nicotine, alcohol, sex, dissociation, daydreaming, technology...and the list continues. Frankl continues to enlighten us that hope was a fundamental principle utilized by those who survived The Holocaust. More importantly, hope is in the moment. These people suffered horrible, traumatic, and inhumane conditions that could have made mental dissociation easy. However, staying in the moment and focusing on this exact breath of our being is vital to overcome suffering. The pain may seem greater but "no pain, no gain." To suffer without pain is not to suffer, and the absence of suffering equates to a lack of meaning. So, staying grounded in the moment and finding meaning through our suffering can help us grasp meaning in our daily lives. This is what really matters—today. Buddha teaches that there are two days in the week that do not matter— yesterday and tomorrow. The here-and-now is all we have.

Let me say that I am no expert in World War II history. Having to describe the previous events felt extremely uncomfortable, but I tried to be sensitive in the language I used, although it was a challenge. I hope you understand that I am attempting to acknowledge my privilege so that I can be vulnerable to the diverse world we live in and respect other cultures. While I can seek to understand differences, I will never know what it's like to live with those differences unless I have experienced them for myself.

Regardless of their race, background, religion, ethnic origin or anything else, finding meaning in suffering is vital for *all* human beings. When I think of purpose and meaning, I am pulled in an existential direction. This universe is full of wonder and awe. The vast mysteriousness of our world and the universe is awe-inspiring. Since the beginning of time, mankind has wielded swords and fists at the sky, demanding more truth; every culture expressed a need for connection with the vastness of the universe. Faith and hope have been humanity's pillars throughout history, helping us to put one foot in front of the other... even when we don't know why. Have you ever stood at the beach staring at the ocean, or atop a mountain, gazing at the stars, or at the edge of a meadow in the springtime? If so, did you ask yourself, "Who made this?" or "Where did this all come from?" What happens when you turn those questions inward, like, "What's my role in the world?" and "Who am I really?" These are the questions your soul wants to know... and many people die without any answers to them. Because technology has replaced spirituality, we have forgotten about our spiritual core, the essence of our existence. Remember, even the grass, flowers, and trees are reaching for the sky for something beyond this earthly place.

They say the longest distance in the world is between the head and the heart. We intellectualize and stay in our headspace, which frames our world from a cognitive structure. Our authentic self lives in the heart space. Imagine the power, love, and magnificence we can bring to each other and our communities by choosing to live from our hearts. Sounds wonderful, but what the hell does it mean? It means that you will have to feel and be vulnerable. It means that you will have to practice the things outlined in this book. It means instant gratification goes out the window and true healing and acceptance occurs through experiencing the pain of your current state. It means that life is not about you all the time and you cannot figure it all out with your genius abilities alone. You must connect to others.

Quiet the head and let the heart speak, is a mantra that sticks with me. The external world and all its distractions prevent us from listening to our heart and intuition. Due to the industrialization and globalization throughout the last century, which has shifted our focus to "more," we have neglected this part of ourselves. When we quiet the external noise, we get the opportunity to hear the internal noise and distractions we have thus far avoided. When you discover your truth, avoiding the truth no longer works. Once we "know" something, we can't "unknow" it. Your personal truth is waiting to be discovered and unleashed!

CHAPTER 7 SHIFTS AND MOVEMENTS

What gives your life meaning?

_____

_____

_____

What creates joy and excitement in your life?

_____

_____

_____

How did you come to this realization?

_____

_____

_____

How have you suffered to find your meaning in life?

_____

_____

_____

What is the hardest moment you had in your life?

_____

_____

_____

How did you overcome it?

_____

_____

_____

How has that shaped who you are?

_____

_____

_____

What is your purpose in your life?

_____

_____

_____

How do you know this to be true?

_____

_____

_____

COMPLETE THE FOLLOWING

Who am I?

_____

_____

_____

Who in my life supports my purpose?

_____

_____

_____

How do they support me?

_____

_____

_____

How can I support others in their purpose?

_____

_____

_____

ANTI-SOCIAL MEDIA

Monitor your time on social media. Research has concluded that there is a correlation between anxiety and depression and the amount of time spent on social media platforms. If you don't want to deactivate your accounts, at least limit your exposure to and frequency on social media to spend the time doing something enjoyable instead.

As you make these shifts, notice what happens: Do you feel more anxious? Do you feel detached from "the world?" Do you unwittingly click on the apps on your phone? Do you feel like you're missing out? After prolonged decrease in social media usage, you might feel more connected to the things that matter the most in your life.

...AND IF YOU DIED TODAY?

The choices we make drive the course of our lives. When we die, our obituary, in a general and sometimes avoidant way, describes the course of our lives and the impact we have made on our family, friends and community. Oftentimes, someone's obituary leaves out the cause of death, certain troubles the person has had, and other important parts of their life. I've never read an obituary that said, "He leaves behind his daughter and son for whom he was too busy to build a relationship." What if obituaries told a true account of who the person was while alive?

If you died today, how would your "true" obituary be presented to your loved ones?

Take some time and write your obituary.

_____

_____

_____

_____

_____

_____

_____

_____

_____

_____

How did I feel when writing this?

_____

_____

_____

What will friends and loved ones think of me if they had to read this?

_____

_____

_____

What changes will I commit to that will change this narrative?

_____

_____

_____

Now imagine, you've applied the approaches from this book to your life.

How will the obituary read then?

_____

_____

_____

_____

_____

_____

_____

_____

_____

So, how do I want to be remembered? What is my legacy?

_____

_____

_____

_____

_____

Now, write your obituary as if you lived your life to the fullest with no regrets.

_____

_____

_____

_____

_____

_____

_____

_____

_____

_____

_____

_____

_____

_____

OUTRO

DON'T EVER FUCKING GIVE UP. EVER.

*"I hated every minute of training, but I said, 'Don't quit.
Suffer now and live the rest of your life as a champion.'"*
MUHAMMAD ALI

Don't ever fucking give up. Ever. There is only one of you. Make your life count. Live your life with no regrets. Let the world see your beautiful soul. Smile more. Connect with people who are different from you. Be vulnerable, look others in the eye and speak up for yourself. Put yourself out there. Try new foods. Travel to places you've only imagined visiting. Fall in love and write love songs and poetry. Write your own book. Go for that promotion at work. Start that business you've always wanted. Dance in the rain. Laugh often and be unapologetic. Do it. Do it with passion and dignity. Do it the way you want it done. Do it without second-guessing yourself. Do it so that when you're gone people remember you. This is it. This is the only shot you get. You will mess up, but you are not the mess. You will make mistakes, but you are not a mistake. You are a lovely human with a kick-ass story. You deserve the world. Don't let anyone tell you that you're not worthy. Don't even let *you* tell you that. Be with people who believe in you and inspire you to grow and expand. Instead of gossiping about others, lift them up with your words. If you have a problem with someone, let them know. You are unique and the universe took its time creating you. Spend the rest of these moments being you.

You are the reason I wrote this book. I want to inspire you to be the best version of you. You are worth every fucking minute of suffering and fighting for what's yours—your life.

ABOUT THE AUTHOR

Henry J. Lucas, millennial, overcomer and risk-taker, is the owner of Lucas Counseling and Consulting. With a focus on trauma, he works with patients in one-on-one sessions, couples' sessions, and group sessions. A firm believer in the power of the creative process, in his practice he applies his knowledge and skills to help others resolve a variety of issues and maximize their full potential. Henry is also an active member of a non-profit organization called *The Mankind Project*, facilitating transformational experiences for men throughout the year. He recently started a foundation that awards scholarships to social work students at the University of Louisville Kent School of Social Work. Entitled the *Compassionate Person* scholarship, it supports diverse students' educational expenses including books, materials, and tuition. A licensed clinical social worker (LCSW) and licensed clinical alcohol and drug counselor (LCADC) in the state of Kentucky, Henry lives in Louisville with his beautiful wife and daughter. For more information, contact him at henry@lucascounseling.org and visit his website: www.lucascounseling.org.

REFERENCES

"Those Who Are About To Die Salute You."
https://en.wikipedia.org/wiki/Ave_Imperator,_morituri_te_salutant

The Alchemist by Paulo Coelho
https://www.amazon.com/dp/0061122416

Schadenfreude
https://www.google.com/search?q=schadenfreude

Mount Stanserhorn
https://www.myswissalps.com/stanserhorn

Man's Search for Meaning by Viktor Frankl
https://www.amazon.com/dp/080701429X

The Art of Loving by Erich Fromm
https://www.amazon.com/dp/0061129739

The Passion of the Christ
https://www.imdb.com/title/tt0335345/

I Can Make a Difference by **Veronica Ray**
https://www.amazon.com/dp/0062553313

SHOUT-OUTS

Shout-out to the men that were there for me early in this journey: Mike P., David N., and Ricky H. Shout-out to all the men in my men's group that have held, supported, and loved me in my darkest times. You know who you are.